# Odysseus
### and the Trojan Horse

Damian Harvey and Martin Remphry

## W
## FRANKLIN WATTS
### LONDON•SYDNEY

# Chapter 1:
# Prince Paris and Queen Helen

The Trojans and the Greeks had been at war for many years. King Priam of Troy was tired of all the fighting – he wanted peace. He sent his sons, Hector and Paris, across the sea to the great Greek city of Sparta so they could make a truce with King Menelaus.

King Menelaus was happy to end the war
and he held a great banquet to honour the
Trojan princes, Hector and Paris. But Paris
fell in love with King Menelaus's wife,
Helen of Sparta. Everyone thought that
Helen was the most beautiful woman
in the world, and so did Paris.

When the Trojan princes left Sparta in their ships, Paris took Helen back to Troy. King Menelaus was furious with the Trojans. He gathered his armies together and, led by the mighty Odysseus, they set off after Paris and Hector.

## Chapter 2:
# War Again!

Outside the walled city of Troy, the Trojans
still refused to give Helen back to the Greeks.
"Let Helen of Sparta go!" commanded
the great Odysseus.

"She is no longer Helen of Sparta!" shouted Paris. "Now she is Helen of Troy!"

Instead of having a huge battle, King Priam sent his two sons, Hector and Paris, to face the Greeks. Odysseus agreed that this was a better way to sort out the argument, so he chose his two best warriors to fight against the Trojan princes.

First came Ajax, famous throughout Greece for his courage and his incredible strength. Together, he and Hector battled for most of the day. At first, the Greek Ajax looked as though he was winning, but Hector bravely fought on. Finally, Hector knocked Ajax to the ground.

"I give in!" cried Ajax.

From the high walls of their city, the
Trojans cheered their hero. They thought
it was all over. But it wasn't. Achilles, the
greatest warrior that ever lived, had agreed
to fight for the Greek king, Menelaus.
He threw his spear and it landed right
in Hector's leg.

Now, all that stood between the Greek army and the city of Troy was Paris, Hector's younger brother. Paris wasn't a great warrior but he picked up his bow and fired arrows at Achilles as he charged towards him. Paris's first arrows bounced harmlessly off Achilles.

"Is that your best shot?" laughed Achilles. Then the next arrow flew through the air and struck Achilles in the ankle. It was the only place on his body where the great warrior could be hurt. Achilles fell down dead at Paris's feet.

Silence fell over the battlefield as everyone stared at the body of the fallen Achilles. No one thought he could ever be killed. Suddenly, Odysseus let out a deafening roar. "CHARGE!" he yelled.

# Chapter 3:
# SIEGE!

The Greek army tried their best to climb the walls and to break down the gates of the Trojan city, but it was no use. The walls were too high and the gates were too strong. The Trojans fought them off every time.

Odysseus paused for a moment. "We must get into the city," he thought. "But how can we do it?" Then, clever Odysseus had an idea. "Build me a great wooden horse," he ordered. "And make it big enough for me and my men to fit inside."

No one really knew what Odysseus was up to, but for many days and nights the Greeks worked hard to build a huge wooden horse.

When it was ready, Odysseus led his men inside. "Now we will trick the Trojans," he said.

15

# Chapter 4:
# Odysseus's Trick

The Greek armies burnt their camps and pretended to sail back to Sparta, leaving only the wooden horse behind on the beach. When the Trojans saw the Greeks sailing away they raced down onto the beach.

They could hardly believe their eyes.
"We've won!" they cheered. "The Greeks
have gone! And look," they cried, admiring
the great wooden horse, "the Greeks have
left us a gift."

Together, the Trojans pushed the horse up the beach and towards the gates of Troy.

Inside, Odysseus and his men were keeping very quiet. "Don't make a sound," hushed Odysseus. He knew that if the Trojans heard them, their plan would fail.

"Wait!" cried one of the Trojan warriors.
"What if the Greeks are trying to trick us?"
He threw his spear into the belly of the
wooden horse. But nothing happened.
The Trojans laughed. "It is a gift!" they
cried. "Let's take it into the city and
celebrate our victory over the Greeks."
Some people still weren't sure though.
They thought the horse
should be
burnt to give
thanks to
the goddess
Athena, but
the others
laughed
at their fears.

"Silence!" said Odysseus to his men.
"Remember, not a sound."

Finally, the horse was pushed and
dragged into the city and the gates
of Troy were shut firmly behind it.
That night, there was a great party.

The whole of Troy celebrated the
end of the long war. Everywhere, the
streets were full of people laughing
and singing, feasting and drinking.

Later, when everyone was finally asleep, Odysseus and his men crept out of the horse and onto the streets of the silent city. All the city's guards were snoring loudly and none of them heard Odysseus and his men tip-toeing past.

Outside the city, under cover of darkness, the Greek ships had returned and the soldiers were waiting silently. Odysseus and his men unlocked the gates and the Greek army charged in.

# Chapter 5:
# Troy is Destroyed

The Trojans were shocked. They tried their best but they were just too tired to fight and to stop Odysseus and the Greek army. Soon the whole city was on fire and the Trojans were running for their lives. By morning, all that remained of the great walled city of Troy was a pile of rubble.

27

After the Trojan War, people forgot
where the great city of Troy had stood.
People aren't even sure today.

But no one will ever forget the story
of the great wooden horse.

# About the story

The story of the wooden horse used by the Greeks to win their war against the Trojans is told in many works of Greek mythology. The best known version is in Homer's *Iliad*. This is an ancient Greek epic poem and one of the oldest works of Western literature. Its written version is dated at around the 8th century BCE. Homer's story relates the events of the final year of the siege of Troy which had lasted for ten years before the successful trick of the wooden horse. The sequel to Homer's *Iliad* is the *Odyssey* which describes Odysseus's epic journey home after the war. Nowadays, we commonly use the term "Trojan horse" to describe any trick. It has even been used to name a computer program.

# Be in the story!

Imagine you are Odysseus when the spear spikes up through the wooden horse. What would you be feeling? What would you say to your soldiers?

Imagine you are one of the Trojans who sees the Greek army burning down Troy. What would you do?

First published in 2014 by
Franklin Watts
338 Euston Road
London
NW1 3BH

Franklin Watts Australia
Level 17/207 Kent Street
Sydney
NSW 2000

A CIP catalogue record for this book is available
from the British Library.

The artwork for this story first appeared in
Hopscotch Myths: Odysseus and the Wooden Horse

ISBN 978 1 4451 3373 7 (hbk)
ISBN 978 1 4451 3374 4 (pbk)
ISBN 978 1 4451 3375 1 (library ebook)
ISBN 978 1 4451 3376 8 (ebook)

Series Editor: Jackie Hamley
Series Advisor: Catherine Glavina
Series Designer: Cathryn Gilbert

Printed in China

Franklin Watts is a divison of
Hachette Children's Books,
an Hachette UK company.
www.hachette.co.uk